Editi

MW00892815

The ABC's of DISCUS

Aquarium breeding guide, reproduction and treatment of major diseases

by

Villa Alessandro

Disclaimer

Please note that the metric system is used as measurement in this book.

CONTENTS

Introduction   4

Chapter. 1   Classified Species of Symphysodon Discus   5

1.1   Anatomy   8

1.2   Distribution and Habitat   11

Chapter. 2   The Perfect Home Aquarium   15

2.1   Aquarium Filter   16

2.1.1   Peat   19

2.1.2   Terminalia Catappa or Indian-Almond   20

2.1.3   Activated Carbon   22

2.1.4   Anti-phosphate Resins   23

2.1.5   How to Choose the Right Filter and Pump   23

2.2   Aquarium Heater   26

2.3   Carbon Dioxide CO2   28

2.4   Aquarium Lighting   32

2.5   Aquarium Water Chemistry   33

Chapter. 3   Amazon Biotope, How to Set Up Your Aquarium   39

Chapter. 4   The Ideal Water Parameters for Your Aquarium   52

Chapter. 5   How to Choose a Healthy Specimen   54

Chapter. 6   Acclimatisation   59

6.1   The Quarantine tank   62

Chapter. 7   Compatibility with Other Species   66

Chapter. 8   Nutrition   73

8.1   Fish Food: Homemade Recipe   75

Chapter. 9   Reverse Osmosis and Water Change   78

Chapter. 10   The Secrets of Reproduction   83

10.1   Fish Breeding Tank and Accessories   87

10.2   How to Feed a Fry in an Aquarium   88

Chapter.11   Main Diseases and Their Treatment   90

Chapter. 12   Aquarium Maintenance   117

12.1   Water Testing Your Aquarium   125

EPILOGUE   128

BIBLIOGRAPHY and SUGGESTED READING LIST   129

A BRIEF INTRODUCTION

For many aquarium lovers the different types of Symphysodon are among the most spectacular and prestigious freshwater fishes; not only for their color patterns, which differ between wild or aquarium types, but also for being high-priced, their difficulty in adapting into aquarium waters and in reproducing.

This manual is to help you breeding this kind of fish, discovering its anatomy, biotope, raising its fry, curing the most common diseases, learning aquarium chemistry and preventing you from spending your money aimlessly, giving you everything you need for the success of your aquarium!

Disclaimer
Please note that the metric system is used as measurement in this book.

Chapter 1

Classified Species of Symphysodon Discus

The "real" Discus, *Symphysodon Discus* or Heckel Discus, was first described in 1840 by ichthyologist Johann Jacob Heckel. The scientific name comes from the Greek terms: *Symphisis* means grown together, *Oduos* means teeth, and *Discus* refers to its body's disc-shaped form.

As a matter of fact, this fish has a particular tooth structure composed of two bone plates that serve as one tooth, for both jawbone and lower jaw.

The complete classification is:

• Domain: EUKARYOTA
• Kingdom: ANIMALIA
• Phylum: CHORDATA
• Class: OSTEICHTHYES
• Order: PERCIFORMES
• Family: CICHLIDAE
• Subfamily: CICHLASOMATINAE
• Genre: SYMPHYSODON

Binomial Nomenclature: *Symphysodon Discus*, Heckel 1840.

Common Name: Disc fish, Discus or The King of the Aquarium.

The first specimens of disc fishes were imported in Europe by Johann Netterer, however only in 1903 Jacques Pellegrin described a subspecies called *Symphysodon Discus Aequifasciatus* (most of the Discus fishes you have seen in aquarium belong to this category).

Researchers changed the *Symphysodon Discus Aequifasciatus* into a separate species over time (*S.Aequifasciatus*) and divided it in 3 subspecies:

Symphysodon Aequifasciatus Aequifasciatus or

- Green Discus (Pellegrin, 1904)

- *Symphysodon Aequifasciatus* or *Axelrodi* Brown Discus (Shultz, 1960)

- *Symphysodon Aequifasciatus Haraldi* or Blue Discus (Shultz, 1960)

In 1981, ichthyologist E. Burgess discovered other wild Discus with a strong predominance of yellow, this new subspecies was called *Symphysodon Aequifasciatus Willischwartzi*, which is rarely mentioned in books.

This categorization is valid for wild specimens, while you can find hundreds of types with different color, shape, and having exotic names in aquariums, but the "pure" wild ones are difficult to obtain.

Just for the record, I am going to illustrate the Classes recognized during the World Discus Championship Duisburg in 2010 that I attended:

- HECKEL stripped turquoise – open class full color
- BROWN solid turquoise – open class stripped/spotted
- BLUE red turquoise – red spotted
- GREEN – red – wild

In the previous World Discus Championship there was another Class named SNAKESKIN which was included in the OPEN CLASS STRIPPED/SPOTTED.

After this quick explanation of Classifications, I will go on explaining the anatomy and its biotope.

1.1 Anatomy

The Discus fish has a squeezed body on its sides, but it is still thick and big.

Watching it in profile it has a disc-shape and the length can even exceed 18cm. Anal and dorsal fins are round and wide, whereas ventral and spinous dorsal fins are long and slim.

Caudal fin is trapezoid-shape and has a powerful appearance.

The color pattern is variable, however for the *S.Aequifasciatus* there are always 9 vertical strips, while for the *Symphysodon Discus* the middle stripe on the side (usually the fifth) is more pronounced.

Moreover, for the *Symphysodon Discus* there are also horizontal stripes.

Regarding sexual dimorphism, you can certainly

distinguish genders during reproduction: the male will show its reproductive organ which has a conical shape, the female extends one ovipositor which has a cylindrical shape.

Except for the reproduction period, it is difficult to distinguish genders. You may notice a frontal prominence for the male and a round profile for the female, also a threadlike extension of the dorsal fin for the male – this last part does not always occur.

However, do not exert yourself too much: the only certain and clear method to tell them apart is during reproduction.

Anatomy of Discus Fish

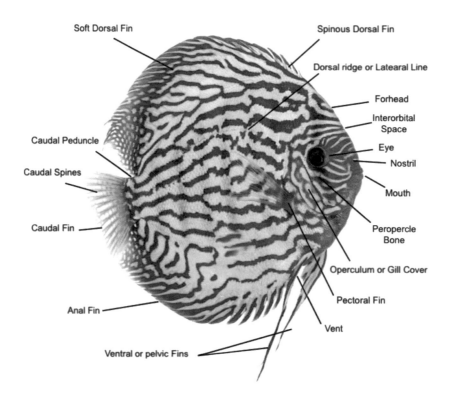

Here below I show you two pictures that I have studied during my Bachelor in Aquaculture and Fish Production Hygiene at University of Bologna (Italy). These pictures were shoot during reproduction and you can see the difference between the two sex organs of SNAKESKIN.

Male

Female

The next paragraph will display the Discus' distribution and habitat and how to prepare your aquarium, avoiding useless costs.

1.2 Distribution and Habitat

The Amazon is the home for the Discus, especially lagoons and swamps full of roots, branches and fallen logs.

The Discus fish was first identified by Johann Natterer who collected the first specimen in the Rio Negro, a tributary of the Amazon River.

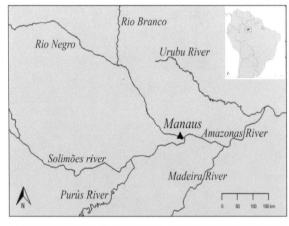

12

In the Amazon basin there are three different types of waters:

• Blackwater

• Whitewater

• Clearwater

Discus can be found in all of the above-mentioned ones, therefore its distribution is very extensive.

Blackwater rivers do not have many sediments, there are only few decomposers such as bacteria, algae or fungus, keeping organic compounds almost intact.

Carbon dioxide and organic acids are high concentrated while nitrates do not surpass 0,1mg/L.

There is no ammonia because the pH is very low and there are only some traces of ammonium.

Blackwater rivers have brownish water that resemble black tea due to humic and fulvic acids that come from humus (decomposed plant detritus) positioned on the bottom of the river.

Water hardness and conductivity are low, as well as pH that does not reach 4.

Examples of blackwater rivers are Rio Negro, Rio Arauca and Rio Içana.

Whitewater rivers have high levels of suspended sediments (mineral and clayish) giving a pale muddy, yellow ocher color, having pH-neutral and low visibility (less than 80cm). The main whitewater rivers are Rio Purus, Rio Madeira, Rio Solimoes.

Clearwater rivers have a color that ranges from yellow to green, limpid water, visibility beyond 5 meters, and a pH that is near-neutral, although they might have slightly acid pH such as Rio Negro.

They flow along graveled and sandy grounds and these are Rio Xingu, Cuiuni and Tapajós.

Now you know where the Discus comes from and in the next chapter, I will teach you how to set up its ideal aquarium.

Chapter 2
The Perfect Home Aquarium

The Discus likes to shoal in dozens, during reproduction it isolates with a partner and is very territorial.

The adult specimens can reach up to 16-18cm of length however I have witnessed some that reached 20cm, they were as large as a pan.

With these dimensions, you should know that you will need a fairly big fish tank: do not be deceived by the small Discus fishes seen in the shops, they do not remain that small forever!

A fish tank with 120cm in length and with 180/200 Liters of water is good enough for 4 adult Discus.

The basic rule is 50 Liters of water for each adult specimen.

Smaller fish tanks will work during reproduction period as I will illustrate in the following chapters.

2.1 Aquarium Filter

The Discus lives in Amazonian rivers with swampy or slow flowing water.

Water seeps through soil and substratum, the microorganisms inside water transform harmful substances into nutrients, these "filter bacteria" biologically decompose the substances that come from dead plants, fish excrement, etc. and clean the water.

In accordance with this principle, your tank's filter works the same way: you may buy the filter included in your tank or separated (there is a vast range of types).

It is composed of various compartments that are necessary for the water flow and allow different types of filtrations – mechanical and biological – as well as heating, and you may add other filtering materials, such as resin or activated carbon.

Mechanical filtration is achieved by water flowing through a filter (in the first and potentially also in the last passage), it traps bigger particles of dirt like uneaten food, plant residuals, excrements, and seaweeds.

For this purpose, there are several synthetic fibers, synthetic sponges, and filtering wools on the market, specially designed and of the most varied brands, which, thanks to their use, will increase the biological efficiency of the following compartments, avoiding accumulations of slime.

In the section of the filter used for BIOLOGICAL purification, on the other hand, materials specifically designed for the settlement of bacteria that carry out the purification of harmful substances and the nitrogen cycle come into play.

Usually very high porosity ceramic or sintered glass tubes are used.

On their surface, they allow an optimal support for the bacteria that are supplied with oxygen and are therefore able to process ammonium, transforming it into nitrite, through an AEROBIUM process.

Their specific shape allows the tubes to provide a structure for ANAEROBIC bacteria as well.

This open pore structure and the very high number of tunnels created ensures that this different type of bacteria has an ideal supply of nutrients and minimum quantities of fresh water.

17

Since there is little or no oxygen, the bacteria are forced to decompose nitrites into nitrates in order to survive, which are not harmful and will also be partly stored in the plants. The special shape of the tubes allows the water to flow through them, so there is no clogging or compaction that could hinder the filtering process.

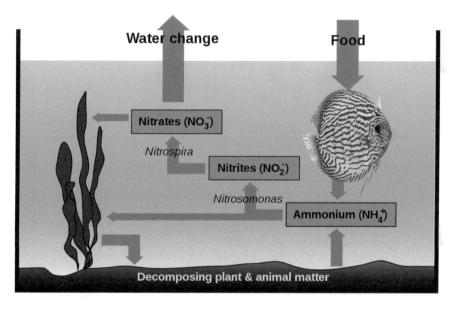

The nitrogen cycle

2.1.1 Peat

In your aquarium for Discus, which come from soft water, the water should also pass through a layer of peat.

It will evenly release valuable humic acids and trace elements over a long period of time.

Depending on the existing water values in your aquarium, the peat will lower the carbonate hardness and the pH value (do not worry, in the next chapters I will explain what they are) and they will remain constant in a slightly acidic range for a long time, giving the water the characteristic yellowish color typical of the natural areas of origin of your beautiful Discus.

2.1.2 Terminalia Catappa or Indian-Almond

Catappa leaves are a real natural remedy for your tank's residents. In fact, you can use it both for its therapeutic effects given its antifungal, anti-parasitic, antiviral and anti-inflammatory properties; and for its properties as a natural bio water-conditioner.

In fact, sold commercially by some brands in the industry, in the form of liquid extract or dried leaves, Catappa reproduces in the aquarium an environment similar to that in nature, decorating at the same time your Biotope, making the water healthier (amber-colored) and acidifying it naturally, thus promoting the typical behavior of the species in the tank, and becoming a valuable additional food for Loricarids, shrimps, etc. …

Some also use it as a filtering material inside the filter compartments or in the quarantine tanks, but in general I recommend that you insert the dried leaves according to the manufacturer's instructions directly into the tank without exceeding the dose of 1 leaf every 8/10 liters if they are small or 1 leaf every 50 liters if they are larger, because they can become toxic if in excess, since the aquarium is a closed environment, and also to recreate a more natural environment and visual impact on the aesthetic side.

2.1.3 Activated Carbon

The Activated carbon is a special filtering material that does not modify in any way the pH and nitrates or phosphates values, but it is very useful to eliminate excesses of medicines after a treatment, or to make the water crystal clear.

These properties are due to its highly porous structure and high specific area, which allow it to retain molecules of other substances within it.

It has an exceptional absorptive capacity, and is used in the most diverse fields, from water purification, decolorization, treatment of poisoning, etc....

ATTENTION! Peat and activated carbon should never be used together.
The charcoal will immediately absorb all the valuable substances in the peat.

22

2.1.4 Anti-Phosphate Resins

Another important material in case of need are anti-phosphate resins.

Phosphates are only minimally used as plant nutrients; too much will cause algae problems and stress in your aquarium for your Discus, and should therefore be completely eliminated or reduced. This material as well as others is sold in different types and from different brands, so you can also create your own external filtration.

2.1.5 How to Choose the Right Filter and Pump

Only through the right water movement can the purifying bacteria multiply optimally and have the necessary time to decompose harmful substances.

Your aquarium water must have enough flow to supply the bacteria with sufficient oxygen and nutrients. If too STRONG, you risk that the pollutants will not be decomposed completely due to lack of time and consequently the bacteria will not be able to multiply properly.

This benefits the growth of algae and the beauty of your aquarium is negatively affected. In addition, with STRONG flow your Discus will live very poorly and less long, maybe hiding in some quiet corner of the tank and causing great stress, which as I taught you, is fertile ground for disease outbreaks.

The SIZE of a filter can also vary depending on the size of your aquarium and the filter media used.

A large filter is better than one that is too small.

Today, almost 100% of the standard aquariums are sold with their own integrated filter suitable for the volume of the tank; instead, you will have to choose it yourself for a home-made tank, also using the indications that you will find on the filters' packaging.

There are two types of filters essentially: internal or external.

In both, you can regulate the flow of water, increasing or decreasing it, by means of small sliding bulkheads, which obstruct the flow of water as far as the internal ones are concerned, or, by means of taps on the quick couplings for the external ones.

 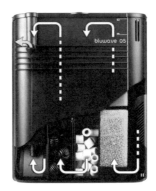

The advantages of an internal filter are many:

• Large filter volumes in a small space

• Multiple chambers for filter materials, heater and pump

• Rapid mechanical filtration

• Slow biological decomposition of harmful substances

• Simple assembly

• Little Cleaning

• Cannot leak water

• Fixes to the glass, takes up little space

• No dangerous crevices for fish

The advantages of an external filter are:

• Higher filtering volumes
• Powerful engine for a long life and saving money
• Comfort
• Practical baskets for filtering materials
• Easy introduction and maintenance of filter materials
• Precise water flow adjustment
• Quick, adjustable and safety fittings
• Mechanical and biological purification
• Manual filter priming pump
• Does not take up space in the aquarium

2.2 Aquarium Heater

Since your Discus and their tank-mates are used to tropical temperatures, obviously the water in your aquarium needs to be warmed as well.

The heater must be placed in the tank, in the point where, thanks to the movement created by the pump, more water passes in its vicinity, or, in the case of an internal filter, it must be placed in the first compartment of the water inlet, so that it heats evenly.

The power needed is very easy to determine: if the tank is located in a poorly heated environment, a heater power of 1.5 watts per liter will be needed; if it is located in a regularly heated environment, 1 watt per liter of water will be sufficient.

Oversizing it will not be a problem in any case, as the consumption to reach a certain temperature will always be the same, indeed, having more power will be useful in case of lack of heating at home for any reason.

Different brands offer fully sealed heaters that are also resistant to salt-water.

The desired temperature is simply set by means of the adjusting wheel with temperature scale at the top of the accessory.

2.3 Carbon Dioxide CO2

If you are a beginner aquarium lover and are just getting started with aquariums, you may be wondering: what does carbon dioxide have to do with it?

Actually CO_2, is not essential in "YOUR" Discus project, we are not making a Dutch aquarium, but it can be important, as it is an essential element for all plants, even for those that we are going to choose to make a beautiful layout, as you will see in the next chapters.

In an aquarium with a properly balanced carbon dioxide content:

• The plants grow vigorously and become more robust and large

• Oxygen content increases because photosynthesis is facilitated

• The pH stabilizes at an optimal acid level for your Discus

• No calcareous deposits appear on the glass or leaves.

There are many different models of carbon dioxide systems for aquariums, from the simplest and most economical to the most complex ones, self-regulating thanks to microprocessors and advanced pH control systems.

They all work in the same way, it will be up to you and your pocket to decide which one to buy, but personally, if you really want to use it, I suggest you start with the easiest one and then move on to the more expensive ones as your experience increases.

NEVER WASTE your money! It's up to you whether to use it or not.

Many shopkeepers, thankfully not all, will not often recommend the cheapest option for you.

Therefore you can find the BASIC KIT to start offered by different brands in the industry in many stores.

In the package you usually find:

• 1 disposable tank

• 1 pressure reducer with internal safety valve

• 1 non-return valve

• 1 diffuser that can be made of blown glass or plastic

• 1 PVC pipe - Teflon

• A tester to see the correct amount of carbon dioxide dissolved in water

In the more complete PROFESSIONAL KITS, after you have gained experience, and you are willing to dip into your pockets, you will find in addition a refillable tank, a solenoid valve and a pH/CO2 regulator.

This kit will allow you to diffuse CO_2 in your aquarium automatically.

In fact, a pHmeter will constantly measure the pH value of the aquarium using a probe and, depending on the desired value that you set, will allow the opening and closing of the solenoid valve for the administration of CO_2.

In this way there will be no waste of gas as the plants do not perform photosynthesis at night and therefore do not consume carbon dioxide and the pH will always remain constant, as a too high concentration of CO_2 will become TOXIC for fish.

Whether it's a basic or professional kit, its adjustment is important. The dissolved CO_2 concentration must never exceed 55/60 mg/l. Otherwise you could poison your Discus and other guests in your aquarium.

Symptoms of poisoning include:
• Accelerated breathing
• Irregular or oblique swimming
• Anxiety

If this happens, it is necessary to make a partial water change and, if possible, to aerate abundantly by suspending the CO2 supply. As you can see, while simple, it can be dangerous to your gilled guests.

Always measure dissolved CO2!

With the basic kit, you can do this with a small accessory that can be fixed to the aquarium glass: the continuous CO2 meter.

Depending on the colour of the reagent contained within, you will know with the comparative table contained in the package, the value of carbon dioxide, and act accordingly on the regulation of your system.

2.4 Aquarium Lighting

Regarding the aquarium lighting, you should know that your Discus do not like bright light.

But most of the plants you are going to put in do. You have to reach the right compromise.

If you choose a standard aquarium with a lid, it already has fluorescent or LED lamps included.

Both have the advantage of being on the market in different colours measured in Kelvin degrees.

• From 3000°K to 4000°K warm light
• From 4000°K to 10000°K cold light
• Over 14000°K to 20000°K blue light
• Special temperatures ideal for HYDROPONICS and marine aquariums

You can then recreate the light you think is best and most harmonious for your tank.

If instead you choose an open aquarium the options for lighting become different, from the most commercial ceiling HQL lights, the modern HQI and the latest LEDs ideal for low power consumption, but very expensive,

especially the professional ones that also allow you to recreate the phases of the moon, thunderstorms, dusk, dawn, which in my opinion, are essential only for marine aquariums of a certain level.

My advice for your tank, if you choose to reproduce the AMAZON BIOTOPE, is to opt for a lighting in any case not too strong, to keep wattage on 0.5 w / liter.

Major would not be natural, but do not worry, I will explain in the next chapters how to set up your aquarium recreating the perfect Amazon Biotope.

2.5 Aquarium Water Chemistry

This section of the book is for you to get a good understanding of the life of your aquarium and what goes on in the tank.

You need terms that will become your daily business and it is good to know them, obviously not as a chemist, but in a simple way.

Total Hardness GH: The total hardness indicates the concentration of calcium and magnesium salts; this directly affects the growth of fish, microorganisms and plants.

Ideal value generally between 6 and 16°dGH, and as we will see later for Discus is also good a lower value.

Carbonate hardness KH: carbonate hardness indicates the compounds of calcium and magnesium with carbonic acid; it binds the acids and prevents a lowering of the pH value, which can be dangerous for fish.
Ideal value generally between 5 and 10° dKH

pH value: The pH value indicates whether the water is acidic (below 7), neutral (7) or basic or alkaline (above 7).
The pH value scale is logarithmic, e.g. pH value 6 indicates an acidic content 10 times higher than value 7.
Therefore, you understand that fluctuations of even one unit should be avoided to prevent irritation of the fish's mucous membrane and gills.
The ideal value for most fish and plants in tropical regions is 6 to 7; for African cichlids 7.5 to 8.5.

Ammonium NH4 / Ammonia NH3: High ammonium values indicate inadequate or insufficient purification of the water by bacteria, e.g. after a water change or a new setup.

If the pH value is higher than 7, the ammonium turns into ammonia, which is dangerous for the fish, exposing them to gill damage and asphyxia. Ammonia can already become lethal at values above 0.02 mg/liter.

Ideal value 0.0mg/l NH3

Nitrites NO2: Nitrites are an intermediate stage in the decomposition of harmful substances (NH4/NH3 turns into NO2). Excessively high nitrite concentrations act as a strong blood poison.

Detectable nitrite values mean that the water is polluted.

Ideal value 0,0mg/l NO2

Nitrates NO3: Nitrates are the next step in the breakdown of pollutants (NO2 becomes NO3) and can also be added to the aquarium with tap water.

If the nitrate level is too high, fish and plants will have difficulty growing and algae will proliferate.

Ideal value max 20mg/l NO3

Iron Fe: Iron is one of the basic nutrients for all aquatic plants. A low iron content is disadvantageous to plants, while an excess of iron will harm fish and even some plants.

Ideal value 0,5mg/l Fe

Oxygen O2 : Oxygen is of vital importance to fish and other living creatures in the aquarium. Even plants require minimal amounts of oxygen at night.

A lack of oxygen causes severe breathlessness and in extreme cases asphyxiation of your Discus and other animals.

Ideal value above 4mg/l O2

Carbon dioxide CO2: Carbon dioxide is an important nutrient for all plants. A CO2 content between 10 and 40mg/l is ideal for both plants and fish.

Ideal value from 10 to 40mg/l CO2, within 20mg/l for particularly delicate fish

Copper Cu: copper is highly poisonous to fish, invertebrates, and microorganisms. Copper can be introduced into the aquarium through tap water or with medications containing copper. The copper concentration should be carefully monitored to avoid overdosing.

Ideal value 0.0mg/l Cu; over 0.3mg/l lethal to snails; over
1 mg/l lethal to all living things in the aquarium.

Phosphate PO4: Phosphate plays an important role in the metabolism of the inhabitants of your tank. Excessively high phosphate values are often caused by overcrowding in the aquarium, phosphate-rich feedstuffs or plant fertilizers containing phosphate.

Excessive phosphate and high nitrate levels lead to algae growth. Ideal value not higher than 1mg/l PO4, but it would be better not higher than 0.5mg/l.

Chlorine Cl: Chlorine is almost always present in tap water and is introduced into the aquarium during a new setup or a water change.

Chlorine corrodes the mucous membranes and gills of your fish even in very small doses. It also reduces the breakdown of pollutants in the filter as it reduces the number of essential purification bacteria.

Ideal value below 0,02mg/l Cl.

In this area, in order to keep under control the various parameters, simple testers come to your aid, either in the form of litmus paper with all the main values to be observed, which are to be immersed in the water and then compared in the table provided inside the package; or in the form of reagents and test tubes, more precise and professional, not to mention the more expensive electronic ones.

All of them are an early warning system that will tell you if the values of your water deviate from the optimal values.

You will then be able to react promptly in case a difference outside the tolerance range occurs, saving time and money, for example with more invasive interventions to rebalance the recreated Biotope or avoiding the death of some expensive fish.

Chapter 3
Amazon Biotope
How to Set Up Your Aquarium

You have come this far, you have seen the importance of choosing a tank, filter, lighting, pumps, CO2, etc.... you have learned some chemical terms in a simple way, you surely already knew them if you are not new to this world.

Now, you will see how to set up your aquarium for Discus, according to the AMAZON BIOTOPE, the natural habitat of your amazing friend.

First and foremost, the first thing you need to do is find the right location for your aquarium.

You have to keep in mind that once filled with water, it will be virtually impossible to move it; just think that after setting it up, it can easily weigh well over 250kg.

Therefore you have to preemptively do some research on your floor's weight capacity, especially if you live in an apartment, but do not be discouraged, with the construction techniques of nowadays, you should fall largely within the parameters.

Returning to the ideal position of the tank, remember that it must be QUIET, and as far as possible AWAY from windows or at least from direct sunlight, since it will disturb the growth of your aquatic plants, encourage the proliferation of algae creating many problems, and your Discus could start swimming in an abnormal way: slightly tilted to the side for their habit of finding the arrangement according to the source of light, this is a detail that few take into account.

A corner of the house or room might be the right place, being away from doors and the continual coming and going of people, but the choice is and should be yours, wherever you like the most.

Let us move on and talk about the cabinet.

You can use one that you already have at home, or, rely on a handmade cabinet.

The important thing is that it must be stable, sturdy and in a horizontal level.

If you wish, you can place an insulating material bottom between the cabinet and the aquarium glass to reduce or avoid the tension created on the glass by a simple grain of sand that you may use for the substrate inside the tank.

This material will also provide you with thermal insulation without heat loss downwards.

There are cabinets for all budgets on the markets, with different brands, design, etc.... it is not an essential object for the success of your project, but it can prevent you from unexpected breakage especially if you know that the surface you are going to use is not perfectly horizontal.

Your ideal location is also near the power outlets!

Obviously...

You have to connect filter, pumps, heater, lights, etc....

It would be even better to have power outlets in a higher position than the aquarium for safety reasons, water and electricity as you well know do not get along, and you will have to be in "contact" with these two components often during water changes and maintenance, so it is better to avoid any possible inconveniences.

Okay. You have got it.

It is time to clean everything and try filling the tank with water only.

This step will help you to see if everything is balancing: the silicone coatings should not leak, you should also get rid of manufacturing residues and dust from inside the tank.

I highly recommend you to NOT use glass cleaner, at least not for the inside, but use only water and a well rinsed sponge to remove any soap: you should keep one sponge only for your tank.

If you think everything is going well, go ahead and create
the AMAZON BIOTOPE!

Professional breeders keep Discus in sterile aquariums, only glass,
for obvious reasons of maintenance, cleaning, etc ... if this is not
your case, the ways to follow to reproduce the BIOTOPE can be 2.
The first, simpler and of great effect, consists of using only peat or
mangrove roots, fine quartz sand, max thickness 0.2 mm, white or
amber color, Catappa leaves and some Alder pinion.

You can add as you like some floating plants such as
Limnobium, long-stemmed plants such as Cabomba on the back
side, or, as some do, put small Pothos or Monstera plants above
the water, helping with suction cup clips, or plexiglass supports.
They will soon root in the tank also helping you with pollutant
filtration and making a beautiful natural view.

The second option, however, is more scenic, and provides
for the greater use of plants resistant to chemical and
physical conditions ideal for Discus.

In this case, you will need to create a fertile substrate for the plants that will help, thanks to its composition, to lower the pH and KH values of your water.

There are different types and prices of substrate, and, from my direct experience, one of the best substrate is the one sold by ADA called AQUASOIL-AMAZONIA:

• It is very fertile
• It does not release coloring substances into water
• The granules remain compact for longer due to their resistance

ATTENTION! Allophanic substrates, like this one, involve a lot of attention during the maturation of the tank, you will need several chemical analysis of the water and frequent partial changes to make the system stable, according to the protocol of the company you will choose.

At the end, however, you will have a fertile fund that will also optimize the values on acid pH and low Kh, ideal for Discus and plants!

Once the 'seabed' has been chosen, a finer grained powder can be used to finish the top of the substrate which will

not only facilitate planting but also increase the rooting of small-rooted plants .

I recommend you continuing with the same product line: AQUASOIL - POWDER AMAZONIA or to choose a very fine, non-calcareous gravel like you saw earlier.

ATTENTION! With these substrates, it can happen that the coarse particles of the fertile one rise to the surface over the finer one, just because of the Discus that like to blow on the food and the Corydoras that constantly move the sand.

Now, you must already have in mind the LAYOUT inside your tank that you want to recreate for your Discus.

A good starting point is a sketch in which are indicated the positions of roots, plants, etc. ...

You need to keep these 3 points in mind:

1. Your tank must have enough hiding places for fish

2. Taller plants should be placed towards the background, otherwise they will cover your view; small, slow-growing plants that will form a carpet should be in the front-row

3. You also need to keep an empty space, large enough to allow free swimming of your Discus

This is the aquarium ideally seen from above:

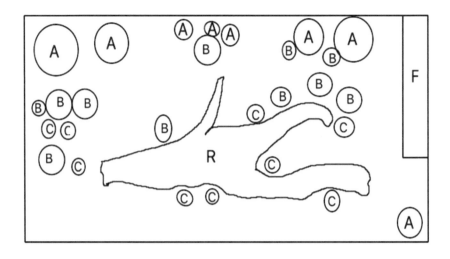

A= background plants B = medium/center plants

C= front-row plants F= filter R= peat root

Once you have chosen your layout, maybe with the help of some videos on YouTube or directly from our website, you should remember that your aquarium will reproduce the AMAZON BIOTOPE, therefore you will have to limit yourself to choose varieties of plants that meet certain requirements, such as: resistance, chemistry of the water, high temperatures and the "average" light of the tank.

Here are the specific plants for your project:

> 1. *ECHINODORUS HORIZONTALIS*
> 2. *CABOMBA AQUATICS*

3. ECHINODORUS TENELLUS

4. MAYACA FLUVIATINIS

5. LUDWIGIA HELMINTHORRIZA

6. EICHOMIA CRASSIPES

7. LIMNOBIUM LAEVIGATUM

However, there are also other plants that grow very well in the peculiar conditions of your aquarium that are not strictly part of the typical environment, but are absolutely no problem for your Discus, and they are:

8. ANUBIAS

9. CRYPTOCORYNE

10. APONOGETON

11.MICROSORIUM

12. BARCLAYA

47

7

8

9

10

11

12

48

Clearly you don't have to exaggerate with the plants, I have in fact listed the most suitable plants, from the floating ones such as No. 5, 6 and 7, to those with large leaves ideal for the center or the background of your tank, to those fast growing and tall for the background.

You'll also find that you'll need planting tools such as pliers, scissors suitable for pruning, and a variety of tools that you can find at your local store or on the internet.

ATTENTION! in nature, Discus live in small groups, protected by mangrove roots, fallen trees, branches and leaves, sometimes in puddles: it is not strictly necessary to plant so much your tank; my advice is to choose the first option, and that is for a nice root or two, maybe full of hiding places for Loricarids, fine sand, some catappa leaves, amber water.

When you get home, you will need to be careful not to introduce any ramshorn snail (aquarium pests) into your

aquarium, and you will only be able to do this if you carefully examine the roots and the health of the plants

once you have removed the rockwool covering them, which must be removed before planting.

You will have to remove the already rotten parts, and

clean the roots being careful not to damage them; insert them using pliers being careful not to leave the root part out of the substrate.

Other plants, however, have the peculiarity to grow on the roots, in this case you can initially anchor them until they support themselves using a fishing line, or elastic bands not too tight, which you will remove once they are no longer needed.

As long as it does not affect the balance of your tank, you should add a ROOT of PEAT wood at the center of the aquarium.

It will release substances useful to keep the water optimal for your Discus and the only one that will not float around ruining all your work once it absorbs the water.

I recommend that you soak it at least 24 hours before adding it.

Another feature of this type of root is to make the water slightly amber colored, similar to that in nature.

I do not recommend adding stones into your aquarium, as some types, such as limestone, can release calcium ions into the water, which will raise the pH value and make it difficult to keep it stable.

If you really can't and won't do without them, make sure they are compatible with the system you have just created.

Go outdoors, wear a mask and PVC gloves, take the rock you want to put in the aquarium and pour on it 2/3 drops of pH reducing solution, a liquid easily available in the store (for example the pH minus of SERA that can also come in handy); or you could use a common anti-scale detergent, if the rock does NOT fry and does NOT foam then you can wash and boil it for 10 minutes before adding it in your aquarium, on the contrary, the rock is of limestone origin and it is not good for your BIOTOPE.
In any case, the shopkeeper will be able to help you
making the right choice.

Chapter 4
The Ideal Water Parameters for Your Aquarium

As I have already described in several chapters, your Discus lives in waters that vary from one to another.

From the very acidic pH of the Blackwater rivers to the neutral pH of the Whitewater rivers and finally to the sometimes-acidic pH of the Clearwater rivers of the Amazon basin.

As well as the pH, other values vary in nature, such as conductivity, which measures the passage of electric current in the water thanks to dissolved salts and, therefore, its mineralization; carbonate and total hardness, depending on the measurements made even within the same area but in different places, such as a river bend, rather than in a stagnant corner.

In addition, European bred Discus live in completely different conditions, and are accustomed since many generations to live well in water with values similar to those of "tap water": with NEUTRAL/BASIC pH and high hardness values.

After this premise, the ideal values of your tank should be:

- Temperature - T °C from 26°C to 30°C (higher during the breeding season as you will see below)
- pH = from 5,5 to 6,5/ 7
- Carbonate Hardness < 3° dKH
- Total Hardness from 0° to 6° dGH
- Conductivity = 20 - 120 microsiemens in reproduction up to 350/400 in growth
- Nitrites unmeasurable/absent
- Nitrates < 20mg/liter
- Phosphates < 1 mg/liter
- Fe = 0,5 mg/liter

ATTENTION! Your Discus is definitely a delicate fish and does not agree with abrupt changes in these parameters.

So, in short, the ranges I have indicated can only vary from one extreme to the other over a very long period of time and very gradually, certainly not in a water change or tank transfer.

Remember this both when you have problems managing the parameters and have the fish inside the aquarium, and when you buy a "new" specimen that you will have to acclimatize in your tank.

The values in the shopkeeper's aquariums can be very different from yours! DO NOT rush!

Chapter 5

How to Choose a Healthy Specimen

The aquarium is ready, the decorations and plants have been arranged, this technique works perfectly, the tests indicate that the water is perfect, it is only missing the activation of the biological filter, which will allow to introduce the fish.

You will find on the market many bio conditioners composed of bacterial cultures that eliminate harmful substances and will settle on the bottom and on the filter's tubes.

It is important not to rush, you need to give the filter time to activate.

Some products may allow the insertion of fish in the tank from the next day, but my advice is to introduce the first "guinea pig" specimens, that are not Discus, starting from the fourteenth day, and in the manner explained later in the paragraph of acclimatization.

Just 3/4 specimens of one of the species compatible with your Discus are enough, so as to produce a small organic load necessary to start the various chemical reactions of the filter.

It is important to dose the food sparingly at this moment, and continue to dose the bio conditioner daily.

A few days have passed and after doing the water tests, which should still be perfect, if you have done everything correctly, you can introduce more fish in order to further increase the organic load and make the biological filter work more substantially. Recheck nitrites, nitrates and ammonia, we are now around the 21th/30th day and it is time to go pick your Discus if your parameters are ok!

As a general rule that you can find on specialized sites, in aquarium magazines and books about these fish, you should follow the famous 50 liters of water per adult specimen, although it has been seen recently that, being animals that tend to live in packs, a lower capacity of the tank leads Discus to assume competitive attitudes among themselves for food and consequently to a strengthening of the immune system and regular growth.

A group of 10 young and small specimens is usually ideal for forming new pairs, but soon you will realize that they will need all the space you are considering now ... so do not rush!

That said, your success will also depend on choosing healthy specimens.

I will talk about their diseases and treatments in later chapters, but my advice is to visit different specialty stores.

In addition to having more choices, you should take the time to get to know them, understand the way the fish are treated by the sales staff, see the condition of the display tanks, ask about a possible quarantine and maybe for clarification on their diet.

More importantly: DO NOT BUY THEM ONLINE!

Unless you trust the seller blindly or you are Expert.

It is too delicate, and the stress collected during the courier shipment might become fatal.

It is one thing to buy a picture, quite another to buy a fish that you patiently observe in person.

The difference is substantial.

First of all, in the store you can also talk to the employee, inquiring about the origin, the breeding, how long they have been in the store, although you will always have to not trust this information too much.

Observe your Discus.

Healthy specimens swim with vigor, in groups, compact, NOT ISOLATED, they show their fins, which should not be ruined in any way.

They have bright colors, a typical discoidal shape, and breathe calmly.

On the contrary, dull and dark colors that do not fade within a few minutes are discouraging signs.

Other bad signs are accelerated breathing, swimming NOT on axis, or rubbing against the tank furnishings, these are symptoms of infection, and you risk buying a specimen that will die soon and could infect your entire aquarium.

If you don't notice anything unusual, you are already on a good start.

Now, call back the shop employee, and ask him nicely if he can feed the discus, so you can see if and what they are eating, if there are specimens that refuse to eat or if the organic waste they produce has a milky or frayed appearance, a sign of an intestinal infection.

After you have seen the behavior, you can focus on the anatomy.

• EYES = must be alive, NOT dull, in proportion to the body and NOT sunken in.

• BACK = must be convex, round, thick, NOT thin, and it must look sturdy.

• GILLS = should be well-shaped and both move harmoniously.

• FINS = should be wide, NOT frayed, NOT closed, NOT dotted. Do not forget to check for the size in your anatomical examination!

In relation to what I have told you so far you should opt for 4/5 specimens of medium size (up to 6/8cm).

Avoid smaller numbers, unless you buy an adult pair already made, with the risk of missing the beauty of seeing the formation of a couple within your group of Discus.

In addition I will give you some more advice: NO fish breeder would sell a breeding pair unless it is at the end of the cycle, so if you can, avoid buying it.

As for the colors, you will have an abundance of choice.

Chapter 6

Acclimatization

Especially for Discus, acclimatization in a new aquarium is a very delicate moment.

It depends on how long the fish stay inside the bag for the transport, the temperature and the temperature changes that can be created during the journey to the house (remember that it is a THERMOFILO fish); from the formation of harmful substances inside the packaging and from the chemical variation of the water quality that degrades very quickly to negative values for its health, very delicate, but that would be over the limit for other species. That said, the perfect acclimatization is the one that allows us to eliminate as soon as possible the toxic substances present in the bag (ammonia, nitrite, etc. ....) but at the same time does not affect those elements that if changed too quickly could cause damage to the Discus as temperature, pH, conductivity.

Always make sure of the values used by the store and once you get home you should:

1. Make sure the other fish in the tank, if any, have eaten and if not, feed them.

2. Turn off the lights in the tank and avoid strong external light sources.

3. Place the closed bag in the aquarium, making sure it floats.

4. Open the bag, roll up the edges so that it remains on the surface of the water without sinking, or, using a magnetic clip or the magnet for cleaning glass in the tank, attach it to the top edge. After about 10/15 minutes, the water inside will have reached the same temperature as in the tank.

Now in about 60 to 90 minutes you will need to gradually add the water from your aquarium to the bag in very small doses.

DON'T RUSH! You will need to do this at regular 15 minute intervals until you have added double or triple the amount of water initially in the bag.

Once you have added the "last water", wait another 30 minutes and then, using a fish net, properly disinfected and rinsed, put inside the tank your beloved Discus, completely removing the transport water that should NOT be poured into your aquarium.

Leave the lights off until the next day and pour in a bioconditioner designed for fish stress, and welcome them!

The first few days, if uncomfortable in their new environment, they may not eat, don't worry.
If the water values are perfect, and the Discus is healthy, offer him some Artemia and you'll see that soon he will be hungry again.

ATTENTION! The Discus suffers particularly from
the famous bacterial cross, an unpleasant condition that can lead in a short time to death if not treated immediately and that can contaminate all species in the tank.
Therefore, the indications just given are to be
considered only and exclusively in the event that you
always buy from the same breeder / store, although, unfortunately, in small percentage, it can always happen.
It is good, therefore, always quarantine the specimens purchased, both Discus and species compatible with them, before inserting them permanently in your tank to avoid the bacterial cross, especially if you want to insert specimens from Asian farms, wild or foreign origin.

6.1 The Quarantine Tank

As you have seen, a few lines ago, the quarantine with Discus and compatible species to be included in your aquarium, is almost mandatory, if you want to avoid the infamous bacterial cross and then throw away a lot of money.

How to set up the quarantine tank and how to behave?
Don't worry! The procedure is simple and effective.
You will need a tank that is not too small but not too large; 50/60 liters will be sufficient.
An air filter, which you will need to mature, a heater, and an aerator.
No furniture, no plants, no bottom. Just glass.
Lighting is not essential.

Equipment such as nets, thermometers, tubes, etc... must be for the exclusive use of this tank, and disinfected at the end of the procedure, not to be used in the main tank during the treatments and during all the quarantine.

The same setup will always be useful for treating sick fish as I will explain in the next chapters.

It is essential at this time to have the same ideal chemical parameters as in the main tank, but with new water.

Do not use water from the main tank to refill it.

After acclimatizing the fish, as you saw at the beginning of this chapter, quarantine begins.

Quarantine lasts from 4 to 6 weeks in the case of fish from Asian farms, due to the difference in bacterial strains.

What you need to do now is to carefully observe your fish, its behavior, livery, feces, breathing, etc., as you will see in the chapter on diseases.

For the first and second week, do nothing except feed the fish a varied diet from the second/third day and observe them carefully for signs of distress.

If you think the fish is healthy, during the third week you can add a small percentage of water from the main tank, but not vice versa, and wait, always observing the behavior of the specimens.

Do this every 2 days with a maximum of 5-10% of water.

In this way the bacteria in your tank will come into minimal contact with the new arrivals, giving them time to get used to their new environment and strengthen their immune system.

During the fourth week, you can begin to do the opposite.

Take a small amount of water from the quarantine tank and pour it into the main tank every 2 days, checking that the inhabitants do not suffer.

After this period of time, if you see that the animals are in perfect health and show no symptoms of disease in both tanks, you can proceed to the insertion of fish purchased in the manner explained above.

To help you with the quarantine, there are specific products on the market, also natural, that you can find online, and in specialized stores.

But from direct personal experience I can safely tell you that even with all the care and procedures of the case, the bacterial cross can always occur, with the risk of losing your fishes.

With the method explained earlier, we can drastically reduce the percentage of this occurring.

A further help to the quarantine can be given also by a good change of new osmotic water that should be "rebuilt" with dedicated salts, in order to lower the bacterial load in the main tank before a new insertion, and through the use of accessories or filters with integrated UV lamps.

Chapter 7

Compatibility with Other Species

The Discus can be raised "easily" in a community aquarium in which there are other species, even not strictly related to the Amazon biotope, as long as they are peaceful, not too lively, and whose characteristics are compatible with the type of water in your tank.

Otherwise, you risk creating an imbalance that will only lead to failure, and a waste of your money and time.

My advice is to recreate the Amazon Biotope as well in terms of the tenants in your aquarium, thus continuing the initial idea of having an environment completely dedicated to the "King of the Freshwater Aquarium".

Compatible species included:

• CHEIRODON AXELRODI (Cardinal Tetra), native to the Rio Negro and Orinoco, it is very easy to breed, and is placed in the center of the aquarium, schooling fish,(buy at least 10 individuals), iit reaches a maximum length of 4 / 5 cm; the female is more rounded in shape.

HEMIGRAMMUS BLEHERI, native to Colombia and Rio Negro, of medium difficulty, it is positioned in the center of the tank; maximum 5 cm long, the female is more robust with a rounded belly, it is a schooling fish.

HYPHESSOBRYCON ERYTHROSTIGMA (Tetra Pérez or Bleeding Heart Tetra), native to the upper basin of the Amazon, to be raised at least in pairs, it positions itself at the center-bottom of the aquarium; males are smaller and more colorful in general, reaching up to 6 cm in length.

CARNEGIELLA MARTHAE (Black-winged hatchetfish), native to the upper Amazon, Guyana, length up to 4,5 cm; medium difficulty to breed, it settles near the surface of the water; the female is smaller with less marked patterns, it is to be kept in groups of at least 6 specimens.

NANNOSTOMUS BECKFORDI (Three-lined Pencilfish) or TRIFASCIATUS, native to the Rio Negro and West Guyana, the male is smaller and more colorful with rounded anal fins, it positions itself in the center/surface of the tank, reaching up to 7 cm in length.

DIANEMA UROSTRIATA, native to the Rio Negro, the females are larger; it is a very peaceful fish and is positioned on the bottom, to be kept in small groups, it reaches up to 10 cm.

PECKOLTIA PULCHER (belongs to family Loricariidae); native to the Rio Negro, in the aquarium habitat it hardly exceeds 10/12 cm, it does not present sexual dimorphism;

it lives on the bottom and on logs, it eats algae, it is very expensive and rare.

CORYDORAS SCHWARTZI / PANDA/ AENEUS / JULII (in photo), defined scavenger fish, living on the bottom, very nice in movements and tireless, maximum length 5/6 cm, the female is more robust, very easy to breed and useful to keep the aquarium substrate clean.

HYPOSTOMUS PLECOSTOMUS, native to the Amazon basin, it reaches up to 20cm in length in the aquarium; bottom fish, it is an excellent algae cleaner.

This species is among the most common, but today there are also many subfamilies of Loricariidae available to the trade that boast attractive colours and smaller sizes such as the Peckoltia mentioned a few lines ago.

Obviously, the costs vary depending on the specimen, especially if "WILD", which means that it is captured in the wild, but I always prefer specimens bred not to feed this type of trade.

There are, for example, some Loricariidae such as Ancistrus or Panaque that can cost up to hundreds of euros, with the risk of not letting them acclimatize properly in your tank.

MIKROGEOPHAGUS RAMIREZI (also known as Papiliochromis Ramirezi, Ramirez's dwarf cichlid or Blue Ram) is a dwarf cichlid native to Venezuela, in the upper Ammazon basin; very beautiful, colorful, easy to breed and small in size, in fact it does not exceed 7 cm, it settles on the bottom. The female is smaller, with red belly and shorter dorsal fins. A note must be made to breed in pairs: it can easily live with your Discus, in fact it adapts without problems to high water temperatures, but it is necessary that your aquarium is large enough, because during the breeding season, it becomes very territorial and could disturb them. But if you have enough space and enough hiding places, you won't have any problems whatsoever and, indeed, you will enjoy this splendid dwarf cichlid.

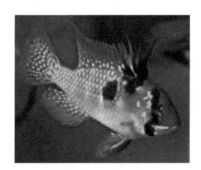

Chapter 8

Nutrition

A very important aspect of your success, in addition to the recreated biotope and water values and that you should not underestimate, is the nutrition of your fish.

A varied diet is ideal for Discus and will help prevent diseases, digestive tract infections; it will increase the coloration, vitality and growth, which you will appreciate by observing your aquarium.

Feeding must be done intelligently and always with the lights on, NEVER at night.

Neither too little, nor exaggerated, but a fair amount and 3 times a day, the quantity should be such that it does not leave residue on the bottom and therefore pollute the water; and in order to allow all the fish in the tank to eat.
Usually, 1 or 2 pinches are enough.

There are different types of feeds on the market, and today they are all designed according to the needs of Discus, just to achieve its general well-being.

Brands are Sera, Tropical, JBL, Tetra , just to name a few, allow you to combine 2/3 products in flakes, granules or crisp that complete the dietary needs of your fish.

They are all balanced, nutritious and keep the immune system effective.

For the general breeding of Discus and from my experience, I recommend combining these products: Tropical D-Allio plus, Tropical Super Spirulina forte, Tropical ASTA color, Tropical D-50 plus.

They are a complete food: rich in garlic, which increases digestion, protects and strengthens the body; astaxanthin, which increases and brightens the colors, especially those tending to red; vitamins, proteins and fibers, oligoelements, amino acids and fat acids.

In addition to the products listed above, you can also add Tropical D-Vital plus, especially during breeding, because thanks to vitamin E, lecithin, squid, krill, it stimulates the development and production of mucus with which the young fish feed.

It was the best combination for me and of course you can find the same ingredients in other brands as well, but I could not fail to mention the company that I personally love.

Having said that, do not forget the Artemia salina!

It has to be dosed a couple of times a week, however if you have little time available, I recommend you to buy the frozen blister pack from your trusted store.

Or you can choose to raise it alive at home with kits available on the market that offer everything you need and instructions for doing so.

8.1 Fish Food: Homemade Recipe

Regarding the feeding of Discus, a separate mention must be made for the "famous" mash.

It is specifically useful to grow Discus even more quickly, very used in breeding, although it is objectively polluting for the presence of ox heart as the main ingredient and then in case of use you must take into account to make partial changes of water as I will explain in later chapters.

Some companies produce their own frozen feed very similarly, such as Stendker, a German company specializing in Discus, but my suggestion is to produce it at home using fresh products.

Everyone has their own secret recipe that they jealously guard but, in general, the ingredients you must have are:

• Ox heart

• Livers

• Spirulina

• Red Shrimps

• Egg Yolk

• Multivitamin in drops or tablets

• Astaxanthine

• Garlic Powder

• Bluefish

• Vegetables

• Isinglass

You clearly don't need to empty the supermarket, but a simple recipe can consist of:

250 g of ox heart

125 g of livers

125 g of blue fish

1 hard-boiled egg yolk

100 g of spinach or vegetables

1 teaspoon of garlic powder

1 sheet of gelatine

And from this starting base you can add shrimp, multivitamins, spirulina, etc.... as you like by adjusting the amounts.

And we now come to the procedure, which is very simple.

After cleaning everything you need, first blanch it and then blend it finely.

Dissolve the isinglass in a bit of water and once the mixture is cold, pour a little (NOT ALL OF IT) into the mash.

You can choose whether to put the mixture on baking paper trying to create a rectangle that you will then cut to the size of 1.5cm x 1.5cm and freeze it or use the classic ice cube tray and then put the cubes, once hardened, in a Tupperware container, which is much more convenient and practical.

The isinglass will keep the food from breaking down immediately, allowing the Discus to eat everything.

Given the ingredients, you will understand that this food pollutes a lot and if you do not want to resort to frequent water changes, you will have to use it occasionally - a couple of times a week, alternating it with dry food.

Chapter 9

Reverse Osmosis and Water Change

You might have understood that the basis is to have stable and ideal water parameters in order to successfully raise your Discus. To maintain the balanced water parameters in the tank, after having seen the possibility of pollution with feed or mash through improper use, you have two options: buy water directly in the store, it is usually sold at about 50 cents per liter, with the use of heavy tanks that once filled are obviously difficult to manage, or buy a reverse osmosis system to be connected to the water supply at home.

My advice is the second option, initially a system can cost from 60 euros up, but you will soon realize that the amount will be amortized almost immediately, saving not only the 50 Cent / liter of the store, but also the time, the cost of gasoline, etc.

What is Reverse Osmosis?
Reverse osmosis is a technology that exploits the ability of certain SEMI-PERMEABLE membranes to separate water from the substances dissolved in it.

Applying a certain pressure, such as that of the home water supply, forces the water to cross the membrane; the pure water, called PERMEATE, is thus divided from the water containing salts, called CONCENTRATE.

The most functional osmotic membrane at this level is that of POLYAMIDE/POLYSULFONE, which acts as a barrier not only against salts and inorganic substances, but also against organic substances with a molecular weight above 100; it is therefore an excellent defense against MICROPOLLUTANT, pesticides, pathogens, viruses and bacteria, potentially contained in the water supply.

This technology is quite recent and is becoming increasingly popular thanks to its simple use, versatility and excellent performance.
You will find both basic and professional systems, the basic ones are equipped with activated carbon cartridges and osmotic membrane; the professional systems have an addition of 5 micron sediment cartridges, with flushing valves for the membrane, with filters for NO_3, PO_4, SiO_2, up to systems that have UV lamps to sterilize water.

On each package you will find written the volume of water they can treat.

The water coming out of these systems, based also on that of your home water supply, may have extreme values of purity that you will have to properly control and make the right "changes" to make it ideal for your Discus.

Provided that the absence of nitrites, nitrates and phosphates is correct, you will modify the pH value, carbonate hardness, total hardness and conductivity if necessary.

Various products can be found on the internet and in stores and they can help you remineralize the water, or raise or lower the pH to the desired value, but you must follow the comparative tables and dosages provided.

To be on the safe side, if you need to modify certain parameters with the help of additional products, or by cutting osmotic water with tap water, always check the values by doing the Test!!!

Below are some pictures of osmosis installations.

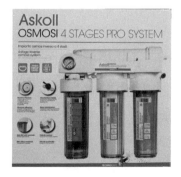  

But how often and how much water should be changed?

The amount of water to be changed in a Discus aquarium generally depends on: the size of the aquarium, the number and size of the fish in relation to the liters of the tank, as well as whether or not ox heart mash is used.

As a general rule, keep a frequent change of water once a week, of around 20% of the total volume of your aquarium.

There is no general rule, but you will have to make your own judgement and observe how your fish react to the change.
There are some people who also change the water twice a day and others who get to 80% of the total volume once a week.

Water quality and frequent changes will also positively affect your friend's growth, but don't overdo it and especially watch out for these two basic mistakes:

1. Abrupt water change: without checking temperature, pH and hardness. Always proceed with caution, pour the water slowly and have the appropriate chemical checks done.

2. Water change is done in a large period of time.

Pollutants accumulate in a short time, and you should avoid changing more than half the water volume to correct the problem once you have noticed that the values are completely out of control. Don't be surprised if in this case the algae will thrive, the coloration of the fish will fade and the plants will not grow.

Chapter 10

The Secrets of Reproduction

Here you are finally reading the chapter that concerns the reproduction of your Discus, after having learned several fundamental steps.

As you have seen before, the sexual dimorphism in Discus is almost non-existent, although some breeder claims to be able to distinguish the genre from the different conformation of the head profile or other morphological details.

You know that for us mere mortals the only way to recognize a male from a female is to observe the fish during the breeding season.

Discus spontaneously form very close and stable pairs, which last practically until the death of one of the two partners.

Reproduction can also be successfully attempted in your aquarium, in your Biotope, and I will soon reveal a very important secret about it.

The female lays up to a thousand sticky eggs that are fertilized by the male and they are layed outdoors, on large and strong leaves of your plants, on vertical surfaces, woods or even on the glass and internal filter.

Here comes now, one of the most amazing moments to observe in a cichlid aquarium: the type of parental care practiced by your Discus.

After laying the eggs, the parents take turns in front of the eggs to move the water, cleaning them, taking them in their mouths to clean them from microorganisms, waiting for them to hatch and, at this very moment, if they are disturbed assiduously and too much by the other fish of your aquarium, they will feel in danger and will destroy everything done up to that moment.

Then observe what happens in the tank without scaring them.

If the water conditions are correct, about 48 to 60 hours will pass from the moment of laying to hatching, and the larvae will remain attached to the substrate chosen by the parents by means of the adhesive peduncles placed on their heads.

Once the yolk sac has been absorbed, the larvae will have become fry and will begin to swim tirelessly alongside their parents for a very important reason.

As a matter of fact, unlike other fish, once hatched the Discus will secrete for a few days a very nutritious mucus with which the fry will initially feed on (at a later time you can give Artemia nauplii and feed powder for young fish).

The substance produced on the epidermis of both Discus is very appreciated by the fry and has always intrigued ichthyologists and scholars in general.

It has been verified that the mucus is secreted by particular calceiform cells and sometimes contains unicellular algae and protozoa that increase nutritional values.

In addition, this precious substance is produced mainly on the back, an area where these cells are concentrated.

Now here is the trick to promote reproduction that not everyone knows.

During winter, slowly reduce water temperature by a few

degrees around 25°C and NEVER below 23°C.

I recommend that you do this very gradually, the Discus is thermophilic.

This operation is useful for the spring where the raising of the thermal level will stimulate the start of the reproductive dynamics and you will gradually bring back the temperature of the tank to "normal" levels nice and easy.

Beyond the reproductive success, this operation is useful for the health of the fish.

10.1 Fish Breeding Tank and Accessories

In professional fish breeding aquariums, Discus are kept in pairs in different sterile aquariums (only glass, no furniture, no bottom and they are sanitized) with inside only a spawning cone that provides the substrate for laying the eggs.

This practice is necessary for those whose primary objective is to simplify and optimize the reproductive performance, thus in my opinion it is a crime to have a home aquarium like this, raising your Discus in an environment completely different from their natural Biotope, but it is good to know in case you will try this method and separate the couple from the rest of the fish.

For these tanks are used the classic cube-shaped aquariums 50cm x 50cm with no less than 120/150 liters.

This shape is ideal for the life of a single pair and allows you to easily manage the fry.

A ceramic cone will be placed in the center and the lighting will not be that important.

You will need just the bare essential for Discus, since there are no plants inside.

Water should always have optimal values and good air filtration in order to allow a proper oxygenation and a slow water movement, without the use of pumps that would bother both Discus and the unborn fish.

In this case, water changes will be more frequent, I recommend you do it daily, siphoning the bottom, and the water should be identical to that of the tank, not to lose all the efforts made.

The water changes should never be more than 20% of the total volume.

10.2 How to Feed a Fry in an Aquarium

After about 5 days of freely swimming with the parents in close contact due to mucus and parental care, freshly hatched Artemia naupli can be fed to the fry every 3 to 4 hours.

It is very important to maintain the stability of the chemical and physical parameters of the water, as mentioned above, until the dorsal fins develop.

After about 10 days, you can start the weaning by dosing freeze-dried food and micro granules specially designed for Discus fry and, gradually, stop using live Artemia.

Now about twenty days have passed and the time has come to separate them from their parents and grow, transferring them to another tank of glass only, without decorations, where you will slowly have to bring the water values to a conductivity of about 300 microsiemens, a slightly basic pH, about 7 / 7.3pH and a temperature close to 28 ° / 29 ° C.

At this moment in 150/200 liters can live together even 40/50 specimens for a couple of months.

It is mandatory to siphon water, with continuous water changes of 50% of the volume, they must be done gradually and always having the same chemical values.
In this period, you can feed the same food and possibly the famous mash.

Within three months, with these procedures you will have healthy and perfect discus with diameter around 5 / 6 cm, ready for a new change of tank, and maybe you can sell them now to your fish shopkeeper creating a profit, or gaining vouchers to use in his/her store.

Chapter 11

Main Diseases and Their Treatment

It is often said that prevention is better than cure and, as in this case, this rule is more than valid.

Unfortunately in Italy, according to the new legislative decrees on the sale of medicines for animals, certain products used for the care of fish are no longer available in stores, but only with a veterinary prescription.
However you don not have to worry, you can find
alternative products to cure your fish in a natural way with the use of medicinal plants from your shopkeeper and you will always have the internet at your disposal for any eventuality.

The treatment recommendations and suggestions I will outline below can NOT be adopted without first testing the tolerability in your tank, due to the different chemical conditions in your aquarium.
The effect cannot be guaranteed as well as the total absence of contraindications due to the chemical quality of your water.
For the instructions, suggestions, or recipes contained in
this book, I disclaim all liability and warranty for damage
to persons, property, or assets.

The "Bible" as far as the chapter of diseases and their treatment is concerned, is definitely "*Handbook of Fish Diseases*" by Dieter Untergasser, which I recommend you buy if you have the chance.

Besides my advice is to treat the fish in a quarantine tank, apart from a few cases, and to get all the necessary supplies in advance.

In any case, below I will explain the most common ones:

LYMPHOCYSTIS DISEASE, it is probably the best-known fish disease caused by viruses.

It first appears on the fins and then spreads over the whole body, leading to the death of the fish after a long time.

It is recognizable because the virus stimulates the skin cells to swell, making the skin rough, the clusters of cells are whitish, looking like eggs, and the affected fish do not show behavioral disorders.

In case of heavy infection it is suggested to kill the fish and keep the aquarium population under control for 60 days.

If it reappears, the fish should be placed in a quarantine aquarium and the main tank must be
disinfected.

The treatment will only be successful if the disease is diagnosed in time.

You will need to remove the affected parts of the fins and place the fish in an environment with optimal conditions and treat it as if it were injured, i.e. with products that prevent and heal bacterial infections, such as ophthalmic ointments applied to the fish until you see improvement and then decreasing the dose to a couple of times a week.

Acriflavin / tripaflavin are also good disinfectants and need to be used as instructed on the package leaflet.

HYDROPSY DISEASE, it is caused by viruses and involves bacteria normally contained in the bacterial flora of the aquarium.

Healthy fish can defend themselves against it.

It is mainly caused by stress or poor tank hygiene.

It can also infect other fish and the symptoms are:

liquid secretions in the abdomen (swollen fish), ulcers, loose skin, fish lie on the bottom or on the surface, do not flee if disturbed, red and sometimes protruding anus, protruding eyes (exophthalmos).

The affected fish should be immediately quarantined, and the aquarium and its contents disinfected. Even if initially treated

92

successfully with tetracycline hydrochloride antibiotics (note: not in the main tank, you will destroy the filter), if the fish has suffered damage to internal organs, such as liver or kidneys, it will die after some time.

FIN CORROSION, it is widespread throughout the world and affects the youngest fish.

The first symptom is a clouding of the fin edges which turn white, the tissue between the rays gradually unravels until it frays and then rots. This disease appears only in bad breeding conditions or as a consequence of another disease.

As a precaution, optimal water quality is essential.

Antibacterial agents such as Sera Bactowert, etc. can be used, followed by neomycin, which should be dissolved at a ratio of 2g/100L for 3 days in the quarantine tank, then filtered over activated charcoal and carried out partial water changes.

COLUMNARIS DISEASE, it is caused by the bacterium Flexibacter Columnaris.

Small whitish areas form on the fins, mouth and the edges of the scales similar to mold, which then decay to the point of uncovering even the fin rays themselves; there is a subsequent production of mucus that causes a difficult intake of oxygen, so the fish will begin to breathe fast.

It can be chronic with a slow course or acute with desquamation in a few hours and death of the fish. The causes might be skin lesions, vitamin deficiency, low oxygen, poor water quality and high ammonia levels.

DO NOT raise the temperature in the tank because you will help this type of bacterium to proliferate.

First you need to isolate the fish in a well-ventilated quarantine tank, where you will feed it vitamin-rich food over the next few days, starting on day 2.

There are many products you can use to try to cure the fish, you can use bactericides together with fungicides, or a drug that contains neomycin, such as Streptosil, to dissolve in the proportion of 2/2.5g x 100 liters for three days. Since this disease manifests itself with poor hygienic conditions of the tank, my advice is to use another tank without any ornaments inside, where you will put the other fish for a few days, so you can allow yourself to make a substantial water change in the main one, after having siphoned all the bottom. The use of a good bioconditioner and new Filter media in addition to the old ones that are already mature, will allow you to add the fish again, only after having carefully measured all the water values that must be perfect.

TUBERCOLOSIS, it is caused by mycobacteria in aquariums with poor living conditions, vitamin deficiencies, weak aquarium conditions also due to undersized filtration that fails to transform harmful substances.

Under optimal conditions, most species will fend off an infection on their own.

Bacteria find space in oxygen-deprived areas, on the bottom, in slime, on food deposits and on dead fish.
It often has a SLOW course and it can lead to the death of individual fish within a few months, in other cases it occurs EPIDEMICALLY and the entire population dies within a few weeks.
The external symptoms depend on many factors and are common to many diseases, they are therefore a red flag: swelling of the abdomen due to the liquid accumulated inside, unhealthy loss of weight, loss of scales, open skin ulcers, lifting of the scales, exophthalmos (bulging eye) until the complete loss of the organ, curved spine, faded colors, twitches while swimming, belly bump, refusal of food, lack of reflexes, isolation.

For an accurate diagnosis it would be necessary to dissect the fish and check the organs under the microscope, a practice suitable for veterinarians and that not even the most experienced aquarists do. It may be confused with **ICHTHYOPHONUS**, but to no effect, because both have NO cure.

N.B. This disease is very dangerous.

If you see a probable TB, contact the local health authority immediately because the affected fish must be disposed of, in case of an epidemic you must kill all the specimens and disinfect the aquarium, but it must be disposed of according to current regulations, not to cause damage or unpleasant consequences for themselves, for the environment and the population, because the bacteria that carry this disease CAN INFECT HUMANS TOO.

Therefore I advise you to always use long latex or nitrile gloves, avoiding contact with water in the presence of fish potentially affected by TB.

ICHTHYOPHTHIRIASIS, also called white spot disease, is manifested by the appearance of whitish dots similar to tiny pearls, visible to the eye, on the whole body of Discus and on the fins.

To recognize it, just look at the behavior of the affected fish, because it will rub on surfaces as if it were "itching".

It is a disease of bacterial origin, caused by the bacterium Ichthyophthirius multifiliis, it is very contagious in aquariums and hardly occurs in tanks with an acid pH, however if it should occur, it can be fatal for Amazonian fish, which over time have never developed antibodies to it, precisely because it is very rare in their environment.

Before talking about a cure, you need to know the life cycle of this bacterium, taken from Dieter Untergasser's book, which you will find in the bibliography,

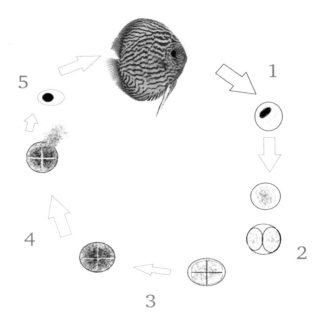

1) The mature parasite detaches from the host.

2) It finds a new substrate on which it attaches and forms a protective and resistant shell.

3) The cyst begins to divide 2 times to form 4 quadrants that in turn divide into tomites.

4) After about 20 hours the membrane ruptures and releases the tomites.

5) Tomites have about 48 hours to find a new host and begin their life cycle again.

ATTENTION! Formed cysts can persist and remain dormant for many weeks!

As for treatment, you have seen from the life cycle of the bacterium that promptness in diagnosing the disease and treating it is crucial.

At the onset of symptoms you must act immediately otherwise you risk losing the fish or all your fish in your aquarium.

Initially you can raise the water temperature gradually (1°c/hour) to a maximum of 30/32°C and maintain it for 3 weeks only if the fish can tolerate it and aerate the tank in several places.

This will increase the metabolism of the bacterium making it grow and die without being able to reproduce in the tank.

You are on the right track if you see improvements immediately, otherwise my advice is to use another product to avoid the risk of a relapse which I have always considered good, it is called Sera Med Professional Protazol.

If you want to try it, please follow the indications provided in the package leaflet: it should be diluted in the amount of 1ml every 20 liters for only 24 hours, followed by a water change (up to 80%) to be carried out in several days, to prevent sending the fish into shock.

Usually only one treatment is needed, as the bacterium does not resist the active ingredient, depending on all the stages in which it can occur.

WORM AND FLAGELLATE INFESTATION, Discus are very prone to infestation by gill worms and flagellates, which occur with clear signs such as darkening of the livery, inappetence, apathy, closed fins.

These "guests" generally live with your Discus, which is why a perfect water and a varied and balanced diet will avoid their proliferation, and a possible death.

I will never end to repeat that prevention is always better than cure!

GILL WORMS, the symptoms of this disease are: accelerated breathing, twitching, refusal of food that may be swallowed and then spit out, nervousness, mono-gill breathing.

The gills may appear swollen and pale.

The cause of this disease is the parasitic worms called Dactylogyrus (or Gill Fluke), which attach themselves with hooks to the gill plates, causing discomfort and irritation.

In severe cases you will also notice a darkening of the livery of your specimens.

But how do you treat it? I recommend Neguvon, a medicinal product for dogs, which is a powdered anti-parasite that can be purchased online, in pharmacies and specialized agricultural stores.

You will need to remove, as with most treatments in general, the activated carbon from the filter.

Turn off the UV lamp if present and run an aerator.

Now you will need to prepare a solution of the medicine with 1 g of powder in 1 liter of water.

You will need 50ml of this solution for every 100 liters of water, to do it just one time.

Leave it for 1 week.

If you see strong stress behavior in your discus, immediately perform a partial water change and wait, also, do not be alarmed if you notice a slightly metallic coloration of the livery, it is normal.

After the week has passed, add new activated carbon into the filter, turn on the UV lamp and do a partial water change.

A mention must be made about the eggs of these parasites, whose only method to be eliminated is to leave the tank completely dry for 3 days, and then set it up again afterwards, but it involves a certain amount of energy and use of materials, so as mentioned above, always check objectively that

everything in your tank is in perfect balance.

FLAGELLATES, they are typical parasites of Discus' the digestive system, that in optimal conditions of your aquarium, can live together without problems.

My advice in this case, is to do at least 1 or 2 treatments per year, as the visible symptoms will be visible only after your Discus will be completely infested, and the results are: loss of weight, dark color livery, nervous behavior, twitch swimming and growth completely blocked.

The most famous flagellates are Hexamita, Spironucleus, Trichomonas, Bodomonas, and they are generally in the intestine, can also attack the blood and various organs, and the treatment in this case is very complicated, leading to the death of your specimen, which in good conditions could just coexist with them.

A special mention must be made of another flagellate, the Protopalina (much larger than the others) which can cause serious damage to the intestinal walls and other organs.

They have the same symptoms and same treatment as the other flagellates.

It has been proved that a protein-only diet increases the risk of contracting these diseases, so a balanced diet as well as the general condition of your aquarium are the basis of your fish' well-being.

How do you treat this disease? With metronidazole (Flagyl) an antibiotic that can be purchased in pharmacies.

You have to dissolve 1 tablet every 25 liters, raise the temperature up to 32°C in a gradual way, don't filter on active carbon and don't use any UV light.

Activate a porous air pump and after 5 days you can make a water change between 30% and 50% of the volume, being careful not to create any kind of shock to your Discus, and repeat the treatment after 1 week.

INTESTINAL WORM or NEMATODES, they are one of the

maintypes of intestinal worms of Discus, the most common are Capillaria and Oxyurida that reproduce through fertilized eggs.

These eggs are expelled with the feces and consequently can be eaten by other fish, which are infected in turn.

Nevertheless, in this case, if they co-exist in small numbers your Discus can live with them without any problem.

The symptoms, indicative of a high infection, are fast weight loss, darkening of the livery, nervousness, shyness and, very important,the expulsion of white, gelatinous and transparent, filamentous stools.

In this case, you should use Tremazol(Sera Med Professional), Flagyl (as described above) or Flagellol (Sera Med Professional) which are the most easily available on the market.

Always stick to the leaflet's instructions available in the package.

Tremazol 1 ml x 15 lt, no activated carbon and no UV lamps; after 6 hours make a gradual change of 80% of water volume, which should be done immediately if, once given to the fish, the water becomes cloudy.

2nd treatment after 7 days and repeat the water change.

You can also use this treatment as a preventative measure of fish in quarantine before introducing them into the community aquarium.

Flagellol 1 ml x 40lt and use air pump in the tank.

Turn off UV lamp and remove activated carbon.

Duration of treatment from 3 to 7 days depending on the infestation, then you have to change 80% of water and reintroduce the active carbon and possibly turn on the UV lamp.

Also in this case, if during the treatment the water becomes cloudy, immediately change 80%, and repeat the dose.

You can also use it as a preventative measure when new fish enter the aquarium in the quarantine tank.

OODINIUM or VELVET DISEASE, it affects Discus and other species, it spreads rapidly in the aquarium thanks to the immune system weakening caused by severe stress conditions, such as a sudden drop in temperature.

The fish show diffuse white spots, are in pain, have closed and floppy fins, stay on the bottom, have labored breathing and irregular swimming.

It affects the mucosa, the gills and sometimes the intestines.

The body appears opaque, like velvet.

After 3/4 days, the livery is covered with a veil similar to flour or sugar, caused by the infestation.

It reminds the Ichthyophthyriasis, but it is less serious if treated immediately with specific products against the parasites of the genus Oodinium, and these medicines are usually copper-based.

Initially you can try a heat treatment, increasing the temperature by 1°C every hour, until you reach 33°C/34°C in 24/36 hours, only if tolerated by your fish.

Clean and oxygenated water is mandatory.

If the fish eats, you can add some garlic and check if there are improvements.

Next, you can try powdered copper sulfate or new generation natural herbal products also available in stores.

For copper sulfate, the basic solution is prepared by mixing 1g of powder + 0.25g of citric acid in 1 liter of distilled water.

The dose is 12.5ml of the solution x 10 liters of your aquarium water, for 10 days, adding half a dose on the third, fifth and seventh day.

During the treatment, keep on hand the chemical test for measuring the dissolved Copper, which must never exceed 0.18mg/l or fall below 0.12mg/l.

You can measure it every other day by re-dosing with the ratio 1 ml = 1 mg $CuSO_4$.

Invertebrates and plants do not tolerate the treatment well or at all, so I suggest you do it in a quarantine tank.

HOLE IN THE HEAD DISEASE, it is a disease that falls among those caused by protozoa as in cases of ichthyophthyriasis and oodyniasis, some scientists think that the causes are of fungal origin, so it is wrong to call it Hexamitosis.

In an advanced stage of this disease you will see holes or cavities in the supraorbital area of the Discus, from which a milky whitish material comes out that derives from the necrosis of tissues.

The symptoms are always the same, lack of appetite, dark livery, white stools and often ends with the death of the Discus.

A successful treatment can prove to be either the use of Flagellol of Sera Med Professional with the doses indicated in the previous paragraphs, or the use of an ointment named Nystatin of the Lederle pharmaceutical company, or similar, which can be purchased in pharmacies without prescription.

Yes, you read it right, an ointment.

Precisely because some scholars think that the cause of this disease is also due to mycetes; after wandering on the internet and in Mr. Untergasser's book I found as a possible treatment the use of this antifungal ointment.

Partly because I already thought the fish was a goner, partly to experiment, I followed the whole procedure that I will explain shortly, with unexpected fast and safe success.

Here's the process.

Catch the sick fish from the aquarium, gently place it on a tissue, preferably not rough and it should be wet with water from the tank.

Dry the affected areas by gently dabbing with a cotton swab or another tissue and spread the ointment on the holes.

Immediately return your Discus to the aquarium.

Although it may seem very invasive as a solution, the fish can actually stay out of the water for 3/4 minutes, and treatment with a little exercise will take 40 seconds at most.

For small holes one treatment is enough, for larger ones, you need to repeat it after 1 week.

It will seem strange, maybe crazy, but with this treatment I saved my Discus, to my amazement, thus confirming the theory of some scientists that the causes of the disease are due to fungi and then to be treated as such with ointments or antifungal solutions.

The most common diseases, treated so far, are all caused by pathogens.

There are also diseases due to environmental or hereditary factors.

In the case of damage caused by other factors, the fish often returns to normal and therefore to a state of health, if the root cause is eliminated quickly, but this is very difficult to discover, especially when it comes to incorrect nutrition, vitamin deficiency, where the negative effects occur after a long period of time, such as the increase in the parasites listed above.

But let's look at some of them:

INJURIES, sometimes aquarium fish themselves get abrasions, cuts, or deep wounds after getting scared and escaping, perhaps by hitting a root, or in rival fights or territorialism.
In this case, the fish should be immediately quarantined and treated with acriflavin/tripaflavin at a dose of 1 g x 1 liter to prevent infection.

Or with a prolonged bath for a few days using table salt dosed for soft water in the proportion of 1g NaCl x 12.5 liters, or 3g x 10 liters for fish in hard water.

You may also use Methylene Blue 50ml x 100 Liters or the Sera Omnipur according to the doses recommended in the instructions sheet, however the last one is not available in Italy.

OXYGEN DEFICIENCY, it can occur in aquariums for several reasons.

Overfeeding, too many fish, poor aeration, dirty filter, slime on the bottom, these can all be the cause of decomposition of organic material, and reduce the level of oxygen in the aquarium.

If you notice that the fish are gasping for air, have pale gills, or you find some dead fish with their mouths open and gills raised, the mistake you can make is to increase aeration.

Don't do that, you will raise more sludge, getting the opposite effect.

A quick remedy is 3% hydrogen peroxide, or H_2O_2 hydrogen peroxide, useful in many cases, which decomposes in water, releasing pure oxygen.

Use 25ml of 3% hydrogen peroxide in 100Liters for 1 time only.

Be careful, an overdose can kill your fish by corroding its gills and mucous membranes.

If the fish's respiration does not stabilize in a few minutes, the lack of oxygen may result from other causes such as gill parasites.

DAMAGE from TEMPERATURE CHANGES, the water temperature is one of the most important environmental factors for your fish, so it is necessary to set the proper breeding temperature as precisely as possible as indicated in the guides.

Species whose optimal temperature differs by more than 4°C should not be kept together.

Digestion and the function of internal organs depend directly on water temperature, so sudden temperature changes could have negative side effects.
The most common and serious mistake you can make is to pour newly purchased fish directly into the aquarium, skipping the acclimatization phase, which I have already described in previous chapters.

The only changes in temperature should be caused during treatments for diseases or during the reproductive cycles of Discus, but only and always in a gradual way.

POISONING: Ammonia, chlorine, nitrites, nitrates, hydrogen sulfide, paint solvents of poor decorative materials, wrong doses of medicines, copper in excess, these are all possible causes of poisoning in the aquarium that can lead to the death of fish in a few hours, so only proper management of the aquarium, its chemistry, the processes of decomposition, water changes and the recommended doses of medicines, can prevent you from falling into dangerous situations for the life of your Discus.

Special mention must be made for ammonia, NH3, a powerful poison for all fish.

At a pH value below 7 it appears as ammonium, non-toxic, derived from all processes of decomposition of organic substances, while an increase in pH above 7 / 7.5, perhaps due to a lack of carbon dioxide

caused by plants following very intense lighting, leads to the formation of ammonia.

Ammonia is very stressful for the fish, if it exceeds 0.1mg/l it will cause damage to the fish's mucous membrane, nerves, and hemorrhages in gills, skin and organs.

A quick remedy is to decrease the pH below 7 with the use of specific products, or with changes of osmotic water and using tap water, being careful to ensure that the changes are not abrupt and immediate.

Nitrites and nitrates are the oxidation products of ammonia and are formed as a result of a high ammonium content after a heavy or sudden organic pollution, perhaps due to over feeding.

If there is an accumulation of nitrite in the soft water aquarium of more than 0.1mg/l, and this nitrite is not oxidized to nitrate, the fish may die suddenly without showing any signs, and with perfect coloration of the livery.

While nitrates are tolerated in much higher doses, even up to 100mg/l, you can avoid their accumulation only with regular water changes and by downsizing the filtration and population of your tank.

Chlorine, which is contained in tap water and must be evaporated by letting the water sit for 24 hours, can poison aquarium fish. The quantit of chlorine in your aquarium is too much when your fish start trembling, they have pale gill coloration, sluggishness and consequently leads to death.

Hydrogen sulfide, on the other hand, is formed during the processes of putrefaction of the organic materials at the bottom of the aquarium, and characteristically smells like rotten eggs.

When free oxygen in the water is consumed, asphyxia and poisoning occur, the gills turn purple and hemorrhages form.

Therefore it is important to perform bottom siphons during water changes in your community aquarium or main tank.

As a conclusion to this chapter dedicated to the most common diseases of the "King of the Freshwater Aquarium", I feel like repeating some basics.

In case of emergency be ready to have everything you need on hand to make in a few minutes your own quarantine tank that you should already keep for acclimatization, with filter, porous air pump, heater and no decoration, just glass.

It is best to always avoid treating fish in the main tank.

Some medications or products are essential and as you have seen, useful in treating multiple diseases.

Obtain them or find alternative products; the internet will help you in finding them. Latex or nitrile gloves, without starch inside, need to be always ready.

During treatments, do not filter the water with activated carbon so as not to nullify the effects of the active ingredients of the products you will be using, just as you

must turn off the UV lamp.

NEVER mix the products, choose a treatment, and follow it.

And lastly the most important thing.

You have in your hands this manual that collects the most important information about Discus, USE IT!

The preparation of the tank, water changes, feeding your Discus, compatibility with other species, chemistry in the aquarium, are the basics to not make the fish sick and to succeed in your fantastic hobby.

Prevention is better than cure!

A fundamental aid to help you recognize a potential disease in time is to learn to observe your fish, so you will notice the abnormal behavior of a sick specimen compared to a healthy one that, as you have seen in this chapter, can be of viral origin, bacterial, resulting from the presence of parasites or chemical-physical water values.

Chapter 12
Aquarium Maintenance

Assuming you have followed all the steps in this manual, the ideal water values for your Discus tank will be those listed in "Chapter II - The Perfect Home Aquarium ".

Here below you will find instructions on how to set up a maintenance plan for your aquarium, what you will need, how often you will need to take chemical measurements, and how to troubleshoot any problems.

With the gained experience, I always recommend that you have at home the necessary tools for any bad situation that may happen in this fantastic hobby, always full of unexpected but also of many rewards.

Thanks to my mistakes and the countless projects carried out, I realized that some things are necessary and they are:

• 1 internal or external secondary filter

• 1 spare pump

• 1 second aerator

• 1 non-digital thermometer

• 1 or 2 water tanks of 30 liters each

• 1 big net

• 1 small net

- rubber tubes
- 1 or 2 bucket
- 1 towel or 1 cloth
- siphon
- timer
- spare filtering materials
- mineral salts for osmotic water
- test
- nitrile gloves

and the list could go on and on....

As for an actual maintenance plan to follow, you can adjust to a cadence of care by breaking it down into daily, weekly, yearly, and as needed.

Daily Care:

- Turning the lighting on and off; the lighting time should be about 12 hours, it corresponds to the length of the tropical day, but in aquarium, it can cause an algae problem, so I suggest you reduce it to 6/8 hours.

I have always used a timer and I suggest you buy one unless your aquarium LED lights already have it, it is used to automatically adjust the times and make sure you always have the same photoperiod.

On the market today, the most advanced aquarium lights with LED technology allow you to simulate all phases of the day, including the moon, sunrise and sunset fully manageable from your smartphone, but perhaps more suitable in a marine aquarium with live corals than in a tank dedicated to Discus.

• Checking the water level; especially when using an open tank, you must not forget to check the water level.

Evaporated water must be replaced so that the filter surface suction works, and the immersion depth of the heater does not fall below the minimum level.

You can do this manually or solve this problem with an auto top-up system, if you have a filter sump with a dedicated tank, or with the use of a special tank, which is more rudimentary but functional.

• Check the filter, you have to eliminate remains of plants that are retained in the grids of the internal filter, or that obstruct the flow of the external one; check that the pump and the aerator work correctly.

If the water flow from the filter is reduced, the mechanical filtration materials should be cleaned.

Also, the reverse flow should be set up to move the surface, which also reduces carbon dioxide loss, creating better conditions for plants and not algae.

• Temperature control; from a direct experience, I suggest you to not use a digital thermometer, you could run into a factory defect or something else.
Check the temperature several times a day to make sure everything is working properly.

• Feeding; feed your fish 2/3 times a day only the amount that is eaten in a short time.

Weekly Care:

• Water Change; in the ways explained in the dedicated chapter, get prepared in order to not create stress to the fish and take advantage of the change to make siphoning of the substrate and the removal of any damaged parts of the plants or their pruning if necessary.
The water should always be prepared before the intervention in order to evaporate the chlorine if you mix osmotic water with tap water. Check the values, the temperature and do not forget to add the bioconditioner.

- Water Tests; the most important parameters should be checked at least once a week.

- Fertilizing plants ; plants perform important functions, such as providing oxygen, promoting the biological decomposition of pollutants and providing hiding places and territorial limits for fish.

If necessary they should be fertilized with specific products in liquid form or tablets.

Yearly care:

Lighting control; the right lighting is important for the life cycles of your aquarium.

Even if the lamps, such as neon, still work, the radiation loses effectiveness over time and you can end up with unhealthy looking plants or algae.

Replace one after 12 months, and the other one after another 2 months, NEVER together because you will change the lighting conditions too abruptly.

A different matter is for LEDs that have a longer life, in this case you have to follow the instructions of each manufacturer.

Regarding the care as needed, in this group, are enclosed all those actions that intervene as a result of problems that may occur within your tank, such

as:

• Excess of food; If after 1 hour from its distribution, the food is still on the bottom without arousing the interest of the fish, you have clearly exaggerated with the quantity and therefore you must remove it

immediately by siphoning the bottom, changing at the same time at least 10% of the water, which you must always keep on hand for any eventuality, such as this, adding a bioconditioner and measuring again the chemical values.

• High values of harmful substances; If during the tests you notice you have high values of harmful substances, the possible causes can be an overpopulation of the tank, the insufficient capacity and size of the filter or over feeding, as you have seen above.

Also in this case, the quickest solution is a water change with the use of water conditioners that also remove the presence of poisonous substances and protect the fish with immediate effect from possible diseases, as well as acting as a booster for the bacteria in the biological filter.

After discovering the cause, act accordingly by either increasing the filter flow rate or moving some specimens to another aquarium.

• Plants Care; pruning or cleaning plants should always be done in conjunction with the weekly water change as I explained before, just to limit the presence of hands in the tank.

Every time you put your hands in the aquarium you cause stress to the fish and you can pollute the water with soap residues or grease.

• Algae removal; on aquarium glass as well as on ornaments or roots, green algae may grow in colonies, but do not be alarmed, this kind of algae only proliferates in good water quality.

The ones on the glass can be removed with the use of the special magnet, while in the tank, if you followed my advice, you should already have the solution with the cleaner fish compatible with your Discus.

However, there are other types of algae that are dangerous and are indicative of poor water quality, high nitrates and phosphates, inadequate filtration, or all of the above combined with a long photoperiod.

Test the water now!

In this case the use of specific products, water changes and reduction of light hours can help you to solve the problem.

• Cleaning of lamps or cover glass; Any limestone deposits can be removed while changing the water using a cloth and pH reducer (wear gloves, mask and goggles), but since you have an Amazonian biotope with soft water, you should not have this problem.

In any case, a dirty glass, which comes between the lighting and the water, significantly reduces the luminous intensity, worsening the health of the plants.

• Cleaning interior glass; as you have seen for the removal of green spot algae on glass, the use of magnets ensures a perfect cleaning and at the same time does not scratch the glasses that will remain perfect for years.

• Fish death; dead fish must be removed from the aquarium immediately. You must also identify the cause of death promptly and remove it.

Also perform a complete water analysis, especially pH, nitrite, ammonia, copper, chlorine and hardness.

12.1 Water Testing Your Aquarium

As I mentioned in the previous chapters, you can find several chemical tests easy to use and of different types on the market, from the most simple and immediate with the use of litmus paper for the main parameters, to those more professional and complete.

The benchmarks for your aquarium, where we have reproduced the Amazonian biotope, are these:

- pH = from 5,5 to 6,5/7
- Carbonate hardness < 3° dKH
- Total Hardness from 0° to 6° dGH
- Conductivity = 20 - 120 microsiemens in reproduction to 350/400 in growth
- Nitrites NOT MEASURABLE
- Nitrates = < 20mg/liter
- Phosphates = < 1 mg/liter
- Iron Fe = 0,5 mg/liter
- Ammonia NH3 = 0,0 mg/liter
- Oxygen O2 = > 4mg/liter
- Carbon Dioxide CO2 = from 10 to 30mg/liter

• Copper Cu = 0,0mg/ liter, >0,3mg/liter lethal for snails, >1mg/liter Lethal to all aquarium residents.
• Chlorine Cl = < 0,02mg/liter

The frequency of parameter measurements also varies according to the experience you gain from observing your aquarium over time and from mistakes.

As a guideline, you will need to measure the chemical compounds listed above on a weekly basis, in order to always have the water quality under control and then act promptly in case of high values, while for some elements you can do it as needed or with a longer time frame.

For example, Iron can be measured if you notice poor plant growth or strong algae growth (as well as phosphate).

Oxygen can be measured every two weeks, or if the fish are unwell (measure it twice in the morning and in the evening on the same day, as values may be higher in the evening).

Copper, on the other hand, should be measured in new water before changing, if the fish are unwell, or after the use of products that contain it.

Chlorine should always be measured in the refill water, in the partial water change or after a new setup of your aquarium.

CONCLUSIONS

You have arrived at the end of my guide, in which I wanted to enclose all my experience that I have acquired over the years, thanks to studies, readings in the aquarium field on trade magazines and forums, the hours spent on books of the course "Aquaculture and Fish Production Hygiene" at University of Bologna (Italy).

Mine was a way to put pen to paper all my know-how on the subject, including in one place everything you need to know about this fish, the King of Freshwater aquariums, the Discus.

After all, I was a beginner too when I discovered my passion for this fantastic hobby, I was inexperienced and I wish there was some help that would have prevented me

from making stupid mistakes, given by haste or bad advice

from the shopkeeper, who saw nothing but piggy bank.

I thank you then, for the time you gave me, now you have

everything you need to successfully set up an aquarium

dedicated to Discus, saving time, money and effort.

Sincerely,
Alessandro Villa

BIBLIOGRAPHY
AND
RECOMMENDED TEXTS

Bianchi I., Mariani M., *L'ABC dell'acquario d'acqua dolce*, Milano,1990

Brunner G., Beck P., *Il nuovo libro delle piante d'acquario, Milano, 1994*

De Jong H., Paccagnella W., *Il grande libro dell'acquario, Milano, 1980*

Millefanti M., *Le malattie dei pesci d'acquario*, Milano ,1996

Mojetta A., *L'acquario, Guida alla progettazione*, Milano, 1991

Richter H.J., *Riproduzione dei pesci in acquario senza problemi*, Milano, 1981

Salvadori M., *I Discus*, Milano, 1998

Dieter U., *Malattie dei pesci d'acquario, diagnosi e trattamento,* traduzione a cura di A. De Jong, Milano 1991

Bernd Degen, Riproduzione *dei Discus, Collana* "Ittioteca" Primaris, 2004

Bernd Degen, *Il Grande Libro del Discus*, Primaris 1999

Horst W. Köhler, Discusmania, *Il re dell'Amazzonia in acquario,* Primaris 1998

Dirk Lambert, *Notizie sui Discus,* Le guide di aquarium Primaris 1995

Valerio Zupo, *Tutto sui Discus, Allevamento e cura in acquario* Editoriale Olimpia, 1993

H. De Jong, *La chimica in acquariofilia,* Le guide aquarium Primaris 1997

Thomas A. Giovanetti, Oliver Lucanus, *Discus Fish* , Barron's Educational Series, 2005

Heiko Bleher Bulla R., *Blehr's discus. Ediz. illustrata. Vol. 2: La storia dell'allevamento del Discus nel mondo. Ieri e oggi*, Aquapress, 2011

Heiko Bleher Bulla R., *Biotopi di Bleher. Spedizioni in habitat acquatici. Biotopi acquatici in natura. Acquario biotopo. Ediz. Illustrata* , Aquapress, 2016

Peter Hiscock, *Enciclopedia delle piante per l'acquario.* Ediz. Illustrata De Vecchi editore 2009

Frank Semper, *Tor zum Amazonas*, Hamburg, Sebra-Verlag, 2011

Industry guides and handbooks are also important and easy to read, they are sponsored by various specialized brands.

Wikipedia

Wikimedia

Different aquarium forums and groups

Disclaimer
Please note that the metric system is used as measurement in this book.

Made in United States
Troutdale, OR
10/08/2024

23574741R00075